# In The Farmyard

# 1

### Can you spot:

1. Which animals there are only one of
2. One animal who is taking a nap
3. One tractor
4. One bunch of carrots

Who do you think the carrots are for?
(The horse, of course!)

ONE
HORSE
FARM

ONE
1

TWO
FEEDS
DAILY

2ND

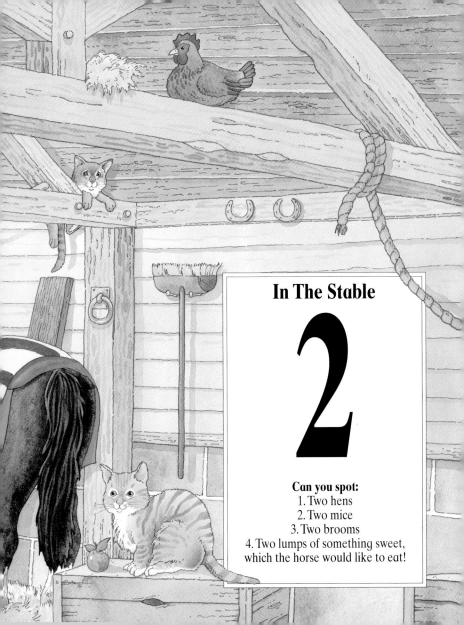

# In The Stable

# 2

**Can you spot:**
1. Two hens
2. Two mice
3. Two brooms
4. Two lumps of something sweet, which the horse would like to eat!

# By The Haystack

# 3

**Can you spot:**
1. Three tractors
2. Three rabbits
3. Three swallows
4. Three tall trees

Can you see three things that "moo"?
Shouldn't be too hard to do!

THREE STILES
FIELD

FOUR
FEEDS
DAILY

# In The Pigsty

# 4

**Can you spot:**
1. Four fat pigs
2. Four little piglets
3. Four juicy apples
4. Four feeding bowls

# In The Cornfield

# 5

SMOKY TOWN 5 MILES

**Can you spot:**
1. Five butterflies
2. Five fieldmice
3. Five ladybirds
4. Five poppies

SIX EGGS

# In The Farmhouse

# 6

### Can you spot:
1. Six kittens
2. Six plates
3. Six welly boots
4. Six loaves of bread

One little mouse is somewhere smelly. Can you spot him in a welly?

JULY 6

# In The Meadow

# 7

**Can you spot:**
1. Seven lambs
2. Seven daisies
3. Seven birds
4. Seven daffodils

MILKING TIME
EIGHT A.M.

# In The Cowshed

# 8

**Can you spot:**
1. Eight milk churns
2. Eight cowbells
3. Eight buckets
4. Eight chicks

It's milking time, the cows are ready. Can you see which one's unsteady?

# By The Duckpond

# 9

**Can you spot:**
1. Nine ducklings
2. Nine bullrushes
3. Nine frogs
4. Nine geese

TEN
DOZEN
EGGS

10

# In The Hen House

# 10

**Can you spot:**
1. Ten hens
2. Ten eggs
3. Ten feathers
4. Ten nests

The hens are clucking in surprise -
They're being watched by
hungry eyes!

# In The Barn

**Can you spot:**
1. One horse
2. Two cows
3. Three pigs
4. Four lambs
5. Five goats
6. Six piglets
7. Seven kittens
8. Eight hens
9. Nine rabbits
10. Ten ducklings

# The Country Fair

Farmer Brown has taken some of the animals from the farm to the country fair. Can you spot the numbers 1-10 hidden in the busy scene?

# See if you can work out these sums

*answers on the last page*

**1.** Count how many eggs each hen has laid. Now add them together, to find how many eggs Farmer Brown's wife can collect.

**2.** There are ten sheep on the farm. If Farmer Brown's dog rounds up four sheep, and chases them into the sheep pen, how many sheep are left in the field?

**3.** Count how many piglets Polly Pig and Penny Pig have. How many piglets are there altogether?

**4.** Count how many ducklings Mother Duck has. Now count how many get lost while swimming on the brook. How many ducklings go home with Mother Duck?

**5a.** It is time for Farmer Brown to shear the sheep. Count how many bags of wool he gets from each sheep. Now add them up to see how many he has altogether.

**b.** Now count how many bags he sells at the market. How many bags of wool does he have left?